'This year journey to that ancient place, back and forth, from Ruth to Jesus, and center your soul on your Redeemer, leading you to worship with fresh awe and wonder at the miracle of the Incarnation.'

Daniel Darling, bestselling author of *The Characters of Christmas*

'This little book is a gem! Engagingly written and sparkling with fresh insights into the biblical text, it led me to worship the great God who works all things for our good and his glory. Read it together with your church this Christmas. It will stoke your wonder and worship.'

Stephen Witmer, Pastor, Pepperell Christian Fellowship, Massachusetts; and author, *Eternity Changes Everything* and *A Big Gospel in Small Places*

'Take the opportunity to hear a different story this advent that will light up your Christmas.'

Ed Drew, Director, Faith in Kids

'Finding Hope Under Bethlehem Skies *is a beautifully woven book of reflections that captivatingly leads the reader through the book of Ruth while simultaneously illuminating the wonderfully familiar story of the birth of Jesus. These reflections will help you to find comfort in the covenant love of God and wonder anew at the Christ child's birth this Advent time.'*

Mel Lacy, Executive Director, Growing Young Disciples; and author, *New City Catechism Curriculum*

'This Advent devotional is a refreshingly different way to view the coming of Jesus through the lens of the book of Ruth. Clear explanations showing how Jesus is the climax of God's love and redemption will engage your mind and heart. Far from being stale and samey, this devotional will bring Advent alive in a new way that will do good to your soul.'

John Stevens, National Director, Fellowshi Evangelical Churches UK (FIEC)

'It's a joy to journey through the book of Ruth with these perceptive and illuminating devotions. They – and the songs that go with them – provide a fresh set of lenses through which to see the unfolding history to the birth of our Saviour. Recommended!'

James Robson, Ministry Director, Keswick Ministries

'Part of the message of Christmas is that God offers hope to ordinary people, in surprising places, in the darkest of times. It is a message our culture desperately needs. Prepare to be encouraged by a devotional that brings hope down to earth.'

Dr Jason Roach, Pastor, The Bridge Battersea; Board Member, The Co-Mission Initiative; and Advisor to the Bishop of London

'Take your whole congregation on a journey together through Advent to the bringer of hope.'

James Lawrence, CPAS Leadership Principal; and author, Growing Leaders

'A beautifully crafted devotional that opens up the Christmas narrative in a fresh way, no matter how many times you have heard the story. The interweaving of Ruth's journey and the creative use of music and wordplay is genius. Take hold of these reflections and allow them to take hold of you.'

Phil Knox, Head of Mission to Young Adults, Evangelical Alliance UK; and author, Story Bearer

'These are beautiful and inspiring devotions to help focus our thinking and praying during Advent. Exploring the wonderful story of Ruth leads us again to the greatest story of all – the story of God coming to be with us in Jesus Christ.'

Rt Revd Dr Emma Ineson, Bishop to the Archbishops of Canterbury and York

25 DAILY REFLECTIONS
FROM THE **BOOK OF RUTH**

Finding Hope Under Bethlehem Skies

AN ADVENT DEVOTIONAL
ROBIN HAM

 Publishing

To Zoe

Thank you for enfleshing
the steadfast kindness of God

Copyright © 2020 by Robin Ham

First published in Great Britain in 2020 by That Happy Certainty

This edition first published in 2021 by 10Publishing

The right of Robin Ham to be identified as the Author of this Work has been asserted by him in accordance with the Copyright, Designs and Patents Act 1988.

British Library Cataloguing in Publication Data
A record for this book is available from the British Library

ISBN: 978-1-913896-54-6

Designed and typeset by Pete Barnsley (CreativeHoot.com)

Cover photo by Wil Stewart on Unsplash

Printed in Denmark

10Publishing, a division of 10ofthose.com
Unit C, Tomlinson Road, Leyland, PR25 2DY, England

Email: info@10ofthose.com
Website: www.10ofthose.com

3 5 7 10 8 6 4

Contents

An Advent Journey

THE STORY BEHIND THE CHRISTMAS STORY

We're all familiar with the Christmas story, but do you know the story *behind* the story?

Tucked away in the Old Testament, hundreds of years before Mary, Joseph and the birth of Jesus, is the story of a girl called Ruth. And at a time when we're very aware of all that is not right in our world, this story is one that rings true. It's a story of sadness and tears, even of death, but it's a story where hope is found in the darkest of places.

Hope is what we need right now, isn't it? After all, for most of us, these have been the strangest years in living memory. Maybe the very idea of 'celebrating' at Christmas seems like a gear shift, given how things have been recently. But that's what makes Ruth the perfect book for Advent – and *this* Advent especially.

As we prepare our hearts to celebrate the birth of our Saviour, the book of Ruth will show us an aching world that we recognise all too well – and yet it will *also* show us that the steadfast kindness of God brings hope for such a world.

USING THIS DEVOTIONAL

Finding Hope Under Bethlehem Skies is made up of twenty-five written reflections, one for every day in December, up to and including Christmas Day.

For each day, you'll be encouraged to read a few verses from Ruth and then the written reflection. At the end, there are little suggestions or questions for further consideration and prayer. You might like to commit to reading the reflections with a friend and then discussing these closing questions together.

Each day's reflection finishes with a song or version of a carol by way of a response. These can easily be found online, but we've compiled a Spotify playlist that includes them all – just search for 'Finding Hope Under Bethlehem Skies' on the Spotify app.

DISCOVERING HOPE TOGETHER

Scripture is best read together with others. For myself, it's been a joy to journey through the book of Ruth alongside sisters and brothers in Christ. These devotions first emerged as a daily Advent email whilst preaching through Ruth at Grace Church Barrow, back in Advent 2019. A year later, when Grace Church was merging with St Paul's Barrow, and after feedback and encouragement, this material was edited into a physical devotional to raise funds for local ministry. Along the way, I've been greatly helped by the writing, sermons, tweets and ponderings of Paul Miller, Mary Evans, Christopher Ash, John Piper, Jonty Allcock, James Bejon, and, last but certainly not least, my wife, Zoe. In thankfulness of the way she daily 'enfleshes' the steadfast love of the Lord, it is to her that these devotions are dedicated.

One of my favourite Christmas carols – 'O Little Town of Bethlehem' – includes this line:

Yet in thy dark streets shineth the everlasting Light;
The hopes and fears of all the years are met in thee tonight.

So as we journey together through the book of Ruth this Advent,
I pray that you might indeed find hope in the darkest of nights.

1 DECEMBER

Preparing for Christmas?

Read Ruth 1:1 and 4:16–17

TORN BY CHRISTMAS

The jingle-filled adverts are on the TV, the kids are practising for their nativity plays and the coffee chains are pushing over-priced, sugar-laced drinks in supposedly festive cups. We're all preparing for Christmas!

But all of that Christmas 'wrapping' has a tendency to divide people. We all have a friend who can't help telling us how 'Christmassy' they're feeling – unless that's you! For most of us, though, the pressure to shed loads of cash, create the perfect Christmas experience and pretend you're feeling 'merry' 24-7 can be more than a little bit overwhelming.

So how are you feeling about preparing for Christmas? For Christians, there can be the added pressure of feeling we're the ones who should be the *most* gleeful. After all, it's about Jesus, right?

Whether it's because this has been an especially tough year, or whether it's that you just feel a sense of 'same old, same old', preparing for Christmas can often feel more of a chore than a delight. Yet my hope is that, over this Advent period, the book of Ruth might be just the kind of preparation for Christmas we all need.

THE STORY BEHIND THE STORY

Think of Ruth as 'the story behind the Christmas story'. Although it is set around a thousand years before Mary and Joseph, we'll discover there are a fair few similarities.

For starters, the events of Ruth also take place in Bethlehem (1:1). There's also the fact that the story focuses in on seemingly ordinary people going about their daily lives, as we also see in 1:1. Perhaps more strikingly, like with Christmas, Ruth reaches its climax in the birth of a precious baby.

But these two stories don't just have similarities. They share a much deeper connection...

Read Ruth 4:16–17

Spoiler alert: this is where our story is heading! The baby that arrives at the end of Ruth is actually no less than the grandfather of Israel's great king, David. And, as we'll discover, this makes him a great, great, great, great... ancestor of *Jesus*.

Is this the ending that you'd expect when you first read Ruth 1:1?

PREPARING FOR THE UNEXPECTED

In a way, we can all get very used to Jesus. Of course, there can be something beautiful about things feeling familiar, perhaps like returning to our childhood home or watching a favourite film. But however familiar we are with the Christmas story, and however familiar we might even be with the story of Ruth, I pray that seeing Ruth as 'the story behind the story' might protect us from an overfamiliarity as we prepare for Christmas.

Take some time to pray that God would be preparing your heart throughout this Advent. Even dare to pray that his astounding kindness would be unexpected *to you in these coming days.*

 Listen to *'Light of the World'* by Lauren Daigle.

What Do You Really Need This Christmas?

Read Ruth 1:1 and Judges 21:25

WHAT DO WE REALLY NEED?

It may just be me, but it seems that the older you get, the more that your Christmas presents tend to focus on what you *need*, rather than what you *want*.

You even see it in the questions we ask. Think about how we might ask a ten-year-old child, 'So what do you *want* for Christmas, love?'

Now compare that to what I tend to get asked. 'So is there anything you *need* this year?'

Maybe I'm just bitter about last year's haul of hankies and shower gel!

ISRAEL'S CHRISTMAS LIST

Yesterday, we had a sneak preview of how the book of Ruth finishes. A baby is born amongst God's people – and, crucially, we're told that one of his descendants will be their future king.

Why's that significant? Notice again the way Ruth begins: 'In the days when the judges ruled...' (v. 1). At a basic level, this gives us a rough dating for when the events of Ruth are set – probably 1200–1000 BC. But more significantly, it also hints at *why* we need this story so much.

In our English Bibles, the book of Ruth has been conveniently placed just after the book of Judges. That means we don't have to look far to understand our narrator's opening comment.

Have a look at the final verse of Judges – Judges 21:25, the very words that set the scene for Ruth...

It's a revealing analysis of life amongst God's people at that time. And yes, we're certainly meant to draw the connection between the two halves of the verse! God's people were without a king – and as a result, it was a horrific free-for-all. To put it simply, the gift of a king was what they desperately *needed*.

But remember what we saw yesterday about how Ruth ends. The birth of someone who will be the ancestor of this king is *exactly* what God is going to provide, albeit through circumstances we'd never expect.

Advent has traditionally been seen as an opportunity for God's people to learn to exercise their waiting muscles. But we tend to wait best – and long most – for the things we know we want *and* need.

We're only just beginning our journey through Ruth, but I'm praying its message will help us to hunger and thirst afresh for our King, Jesus. This gift of a King in the midst of all the mess of life is the most spectacular display of God's kindness. A kindness that, God willing, won't leave us unchanged.

> *Pray that God would help you rediscover your own need of this King, born in a manger and under Bethlehem skies. Pray that our hearts, naturally bent on doing 'as we see fit', would instead be open to trusting in Jesus' kind and royal rule.*

Listen to *'O Come, All You Unfaithful'* by Sovereign Grace Music.

3 DECEMBER

Escaping Advent?

Read Ruth 1:1–2

THE CUPBOARDS ARE BARE

Christmas is often portrayed as a time of feasting: platefuls of mince pies, chocolate supplies in every room, turkey with all the trimmings…

The beginning of Ruth therefore feels like quite a gear change: '…there was a famine in the land' (v. 1). But if we linger here, we'll see this opening has an important – and even *refreshing* – word for us.

'Land' here refers to Israel and Judah, the place of blessing that God had promised to Abraham and his descendants. So why was there a famine?

WARNING LIGHTS

We need to read between the lines here. We saw yesterday that God's people were on a downward spiral of disobedience and idolatry (Ruth 1:1 and Judges 21:25). But the news of a 'famine' is further evidence things have gone awry spiritually. The Old Testament law included clear consequences if God's people turned away to false gods. Significantly, one of these consequences was famine (see Deuteronomy 28:15–29).

In other words, this national widespread hunger should have been a warning light flashing on Israel's dashboard. It meant all was not well with their relationship with God.

And like all warning lights, it was meant to evoke a response…

MEET THE FAMILY

As we're introduced to the people in this story, it's notable that the very first details given are not their names, characters or occupations. Instead, it's *where they're from* – Bethlehem – and *where they're going* – Moab. To put it another way, we're told their *response* to the famine. And despite first impressions, these locations reveal a particularly unwise response.

Firstly, Bethlehem was part of God's promised land. Its name literally meant 'house of bread'. But Moab, on the other hand, was one of the long-standing enemies of God's people. The first readers of this story would have therefore raised their eyebrows: 'You're going where? To *Moab*?!'

Both places are then repeated for emphasis in verse 2, sandwiching the family's names: 'They were Ephrathites from Bethlehem, Judah. And they went to Moab and lived there.'

Now, we might think, 'Aren't they just doing what anyone would have done in that situation?' But remember that this was no ordinary famine. It was a God-given warning light urging God's people to turn to him in repentance. It certainly wasn't an invitation to flee further away!

DENIAL STRATEGIES

But isn't this what we do? Essentially, Elimelek and Naomi's actions are just one little example of how we respond when confronted with the reality of a fractured relationship with God. When faced with our brokenness and depravity, it's all too easy to turn away.

All this might not seem very Christmassy! But traditionally, Advent is understood as an opportunity to face up to the darkness in order to appreciate the light.

Maybe our culture's desire to 'bring Christmas in early' is symptomatic of trying to escape the reality of our brokenness?[1] Yet no one can escape reality for long. In a world that aches with sin, pretending everything is endless cheer is both deceptive *and* exhausting.

> *Things aren't as they should be – globally, nationally, but also personally. Take some time to confess your own sin. Do you seek to 'escape' from this reality? Give thanks that God's word is honest about the brokenness of our aching world. How could this inspire conversations you have today?*
>
> Listen to *'Deliver Us'* by Andrew Peterson.

[1.] I owe this point to Tish Harrison Warren in her article, 'Want to Get into the Christmas Spirit? Face the Darkness' (The New York Times, 30 November 2019), https://www.nytimes.com/2019/11/30/opinion/sunday/christmas-season-advent-celebration.html

Driving Home for Christmas

Read Ruth 1:3–10

THE LONGEST JOURNEY

Where will you be travelling this Christmas? Whether it's overdue catch-ups with friends or long trips to see far-flung relatives, we're used to meaningful journeys at this time of year.

Yesterday, Elimelek, Naomi and their two sons made a journey from Bethlehem to Moab. But things don't turn out the way they hoped.

Within just ten years of arriving in Moab, Naomi had faced three family funerals, losing her husband and both of her sons (vv. 3, 5). It's hard to imagine such grief. And for a woman in that culture, it meant she'd lost *everything*: status, security, provision. Moab had promised life, but brought only death.

It was time to return home.

TURNING BACK

Naomi's decision to return seems initially prompted by news that Bethlehem's famine is over: 'the LORD had come to the aid of his people by providing food for them' (v. 6).

But she may not return alone. Her sons had each married Moabite girls, Orpah and Ruth. The rest of the chapter unpacks an incredibly moving conversation between the three of them as Naomi tries to convince her daughters-in-law to remain in their homeland.

Strikingly, the Hebrew verb 'to return or turn' occurs twelve times in this dialogue (though not all show in our English translations).

WHERE KINDNESS IS FOUND

We're being shown that Naomi isn't just going on a *physical* journey. As we'll see, this book is all about her spiritual journey, as she rediscovers who the Lord really is.

For example, Naomi seems spiritually confused in chapter 1. She is hopeful that Ruth and Orpah will experience the Lord's 'kindness' in Moab (v. 8). But this Hebrew word, *hesed*, spoke of God's special covenant love. Any self-respecting Israelite would know that the place of God's covenant blessing was Israel, not Moab!

And does Naomi really expect her daughters-in-law to find 'rest in the home of another husband', as she says in verse 9? After all, that certainly hadn't been Naomi's experience.

HOPE IN BETHLEHEM

But Naomi's journey is one with which many of us will identify. We can all find it difficult to rest in God's promises. We all have seasons of struggling to trust God is for us. And so the repeated language of 'turning' gently encourages us to consider which direction *we* are turned: towards Moab or Bethlehem?

As Naomi turns back to Bethlehem, she is actually turning back to the Lord, the God of steadfast kindness. So what journey have you been on this year? And which direction are you now facing?

For Christians, every day is full of countless 'little' moments of turning away from God. That's why daily habits that help us turn back 'home' to Christ in repentance and faith are so important.

But maybe we're in a season where we've been persistently looking for hope in the wrong places? These verses invite us to return from 'Moab' and find hope and life in Jesus Christ, the perfect expression of God's loving kindness. It's time to come home.

How do you need to turn back from 'Moab' at the moment? Where are you searching vainly for a false hope? Pray that as you prepare for Christmas, your heart would be daily turned towards Christ as your source of hope and rest.

Listen to *'There Blooms a Rose in Bethlehem'* by Sovereign Grace Music.

Loved, Actually

Read Ruth 1:11–14

I WANNA KNOW WHAT LOVE IS

What's your pick for the greatest Christmas movie of all time? Don't judge me, but one of my favourites is *Love Actually*, actually! It's mainly because the year it was released, I was preparing to leave home for six months overseas. Unsurprisingly, the film's opening scene at the arrivals gate of Heathrow Airport has bittersweet memories!

But to the credit of writer and director Richard Curtis, it's a romcom that manages to capture a fairly rich and honest portrait of human love. We see that love in its many forms and distortions: quiet devotion, consuming self-love, longing grief, besotted romance, destructive lust, brave loyalty…

We love the idea of love, especially at Christmas. In today's passage in Ruth, we begin to see a demonstration of love that Hollywood scriptwriters would die for.

HOPELESS HEARTACHE

Grieving Naomi believes her widowed daughters-in-law should stay in their homeland, rather than accompany her to Bethlehem. Part of her reasoning is that she is 'too old to have another husband … even if I had a husband tonight and then gave birth to sons – would you wait until they grew up?' (vv. 12–13).

This is a reference to the custom of levirate marriage, where the bereaved woman would be cared for through existing family relationships. For example, if a married man died, his brother would be expected to marry his widow. That might sound like a social nightmare to us, but it ensured both that the widow was provided for *and* that the deceased husband's land was passed on to the next generation.

But Naomi knows the idea of remarrying and then giving birth to sons who *in turn* could marry Ruth and Orpah is fool's talk. She's simply too old for this (v. 13)! She believes her situation to be hopeless and therefore urges her daughters-in-law to cut their losses.

In fact, look how Naomi describes God's role in this situation: '... the LORD's hand has turned against me!' (v. 13).

KINDNESS ENFLESHED

It's commendable that Naomi believes God is in control of all things, but is the Lord really *against* her?

Notably, Naomi makes this declaration on two occasions in this chapter (vv. 13, 20), and each time it seems that God responds to Naomi's remark. This doesn't take the form of direct speech, but is through the events and responses of other people. For example, look at what happens directly after Naomi's first remark: 'Then Orpah kissed her mother-in-law goodbye, *but Ruth clung to her*' (v. 14, my italics)

Naomi is on a journey of rediscovering the Lord's steadfast kindness, but the way that she'll discover this kindness is as she experiences it embodied in the actions of other individuals. In today's passage, it's particularly Ruth who 'enfleshes' that covenant kindness, literally enwrapping herself around Naomi in sacrificial commitment.

In Advent, we prepare to celebrate God embodying his kindness to us in Jesus Christ. Do you need to be convinced that God is for you? If you're honest, are there things that lead you to feeling that the Lord's hand is 'turned against' you? As you picture Ruth clinging to Naomi, let your heart be reconvinced that God will not let you go. Pray for the Lord's help as you entrust yourself to his love for you.

 Listen to *'Love's Coming Down'* by Melanie Penn.

Wherever You Will Go

Read Ruth 1:15–18

LOVE DECLARED

What difference does it make to know that you're loved?

Poor Naomi is preparing to return to her homeland alone. But whilst she believes her daughters-in-law should part ways with her, one of them isn't so sure. Instead of letting go, Ruth shows a dogged commitment in holding tight to her stricken mother-in-law. Why?

Today, we see Naomi again trying to persuade Ruth to follow her sister-in-law, Orpah, and turn back to Moab. As Naomi reminds Ruth, Orpah has already decided to return 'to her people and her gods'. According to Naomi, Ruth should do likewise: 'Go back with her' (v. 15).

But upon reflection, Naomi's plea is a rather strange one. After all, why would a faithful Israelite encourage someone to carry on worshipping their false gods?

Tragically, it seems Naomi's comment was typical of God's people during the time of the book of Judges. People believed they could *combine* worshipping the Lord with worshipping the false gods of neighbouring nations.

RESTING IN THE ONE TRUE GOD

Strikingly, it seems that Ruth has a clearer grasp on who God is than Naomi. It's as if Naomi's comment crystallises for Ruth her own decision to stick with Naomi. As a consequence, we're given one of the most stunning declarations of love that you'll ever read in a piece of literature:

> *Where you go I will go, and where you stay I will stay. Your people will be my people and your God my God. Where you die I will die, and there I will be buried (vv. 16–17).*

Together, these three sentences form a beautiful expression of *hesed*, the Hebrew word for God's covenant love. Unsurprisingly, it leaves Naomi speechless (v. 18).

What are we to make of Ruth's breathtaking declaration? What prompts her to show such staggering kindness?

ENTRUSTED TO THE LORD

It's important to see that this pledge isn't just about Ruth's relationship with and commitment to Naomi. If it was, then why would Ruth commit to staying in Naomi's land beyond Naomi's death? Rather, the motivation for Ruth's love for Naomi is a much more important relationship: Ruth's relationship with and commitment to the Lord. As Paul Miller notes, 'The form of Ruth's poem, with God at the centre, mirrors the shape of her heart.'[2]

In that culture, it was unthinkable to change your religion or citizenship. You just *didn't* do that. But Ruth has already done both.

And we assume that these weren't changes that Ruth had simply made in the moment. Over the years, she'd have learnt about the Lord's character and grace-filled promises, not least through the daily rhythms, behaviour and conversations of Naomi and her sons.

So we can imagine that Ruth gradually came to a point where she knew 'the LORD, the compassionate and gracious God, slow to anger,

---

[2] Paul Miller, *A Loving Life* (revised edition: Tyndale House Publishers, 2017), p. 38.

abounding in love and faithfulness' (Exodus 34:6) was the God to whom she *could* entrust her life.

And when you're certain of the Lord's love for you, that changes *everything*. As Naomi's trust in God now faltered, Ruth had the opportunity to demonstrate God's radical *hesed* love back to her mother-in-law.

Imagine this scene on the road to Bethlehem. How do you feel as you hear Ruth uttering these words to Naomi? What does it remind you of? In Jesus, God speaks these very words to you. What does that change for you? Spend some time reflecting on how you might show this kind of covenant love this Advent.

 Listen to *'May You Find a Light'* by Josh Garrels.

Living Bread for Empty Hearts

Read Ruth 1:19–22

TELL ME HOW YOUR YEAR'S BEEN!

Have you ever had one of those moments at a Christmas get-together when a friend or family member has asked, 'So how's it going with you?' and you've just not known where to start? Do you share surface-level news, or choose to open up a bit deeper? Should you give the Instagram-filtered 'highlights reel', or the behind-the-scenes reality?

As Naomi returns to Bethlehem and is reacquainted with forgotten faces, today's passage invites us to reflect on the bigger question of what God is doing in our lives.

I HARDLY RECOGNISED YOU

Just as in 1:1–3, the name *Bethlehem* is repeated to indicate the spiritual significance of Naomi's return (twice in verse 19 and again in verse 22). Having turned from the Lord towards Moab, Naomi has now returned to the land of promise and hope.

But those who greet Naomi find her unrecognisable: 'Can this be Naomi?' (v. 19). There is a tragic irony here. Naomi's name means 'pleasant' in Hebrew (read the footnote to verse 20), but as the women see Naomi's whole demeanour, her face tells a very different story.

As the word 'pleasant' literally echoes in the air with the women's question, Naomi can't stand it. She cries out, 'Call me Mara', which is Hebrew for 'bitter'. Why? '… because the Almighty has made my life very bitter' (v. 20).

EMPTINESS PERSONIFIED?

Naomi isn't holding back. As she puts it, 'I went away full, but the LORD has brought me back empty' (v. 21). This is a woman who has buried her husband and two sons. If anyone had a right to feel 'empty', surely it was her. And yet...

Just like when Naomi made a similarly forlorn remark in verse 13, the narrator gives us a rather different angle: 'So Naomi returned from Moab *accompanied by Ruth* … arriving in Bethlehem *as the barley harvest was beginning*' (v. 22, my italics).

Yes, what Naomi has gone through is unimaginable for most of us, but has the Lord really brought her back *empty*?

LOOK AND SEE WHAT THE LORD HAS DONE

As someone observed, it's as if Naomi has announced the verdict before she's seen all the evidence. And in particular, there's a crucial piece of evidence that she's missed right in front of her nose: Ruth.

In Ruth, Naomi has a visible pledge of God's unending commitment to her. Not only that, but look what's happening in the fields of Bethlehem. It's harvest time!

A chapter that began with famine in the 'house of bread' (for that is what 'Bethlehem' means) has finished with a harvest. Hope has come to Bethlehem.

THE BREAD OF LIFE GIVEN FOR US

Of course, just like Naomi, it's easy for us to become absorbed in our circumstances. We struggle to lift our eyes to the bigger picture.

Reassuringly, this book never belittles the bitterness of Naomi's suffering. And throughout the Bible, we are certainly encouraged to be honest with God about our trials and struggles.

But as real as Naomi's emptiness felt, Ruth's presence with her is a demonstration of the Lord's faithful presence. He has *not* left her, nor turned his hand against her.

This story is only just getting started. And for us, it's part of a bigger story that leads us back to Bethlehem. A thousand years later, hope will return again to this little town. A spiritual famine will end as the Bread of Life is given for us.

Are you ever tempted to say your life is 'empty'? Whatever painful realities we might face, as we turn and look alongside us, we see One who will never leave us, One who has been broken for us, and One who will wipe each bitter tear from our eyes. When we count our blessings, how much do we count Christ?

Listen to *'O Little Town of Bethlehem'* by Young Oceans.

As Chance Would Have It?

Read Ruth 2:1–3

HOPE ON THE HORIZON?

There's a sense of hope in the air in Bethlehem. After desperate beginnings, Naomi is back in Bethlehem – and Ruth is alongside her. The narrator now gives us some important information: 'Naomi had a relative on her husband's side, a man of standing from the clan of Elimelek, whose name was Boaz' (v. 1).

In a short little book like Ruth, words aren't wasted. This news should make our ears prick up. Why? As we saw previously, widows were to be looked after by their dead husband's extended family (see Deuteronomy 25:5–10). So the news that Naomi has a relative on her husband's side is very significant. Even better, he is a 'man of standing'. This bodes well!

But how will Naomi find him? And what will his response be?

HOPELESSLY DEVOTED

With no other means of income, and no inheritance in the land, Naomi and Ruth's prospects seem otherwise pretty bleak – so much so that Ruth offers to go and glean leftover grain in the fields (v. 2).

Landowners were commanded by God to leave the edges of their fields unharvested so that foreigners, the fatherless and widows could glean a harvest for themselves (see Deuteronomy 24:19–21). But this was a humbling prospect, perhaps akin to trawling through waste bins for scraps of food.

And remember that this was a time when 'everyone did as they saw fit' (Judges 21:25). Who knew what trouble a vulnerable woman would run into if she went foraging for food alone.

THE GOD OF GOD-INCIDENCES

If verse 1 made our ears prick up, verse 3 should make our eyes widen – and prompt a wry smile: 'As it turned out, [Ruth] was working in a field belonging to Boaz, who was from the clan of Elimelek' (v. 3).

'As it turned out'?! Of all the fields in Bethlehem, which one does Ruth wander into first? A field belonging to Boaz, the one man who might be able to do something about Naomi and Ruth's sorry situation.

But as we see throughout this book, nothing just 'turns out'. This is a world created, sustained and ordered by a God who does not fail to look after his people. A God who ensures Ruth doesn't end up in Billy's field or Barry's field, but in Boaz's field.

NOTHING MORE THAN GOD'S GOODNESS IN ACTION

This truth is sometimes called God's 'providence'. Every event – including human thoughts, choices and actions – occurs according to God's sovereign will.

Of course, whether this is an attractive thought depends upon God's character. But if God is utterly and graciously committed to his people, what could be more reassuring? That's why Charles Spurgeon described God's providence as 'nothing more than his goodness in action'.[3]

[3.] Charles Spurgeon, 'God's Hand and Providence to Be Religiously Acknowledged in Public Calamities: A Sermon Occasioned by the Great Fire in Boston, New England, Thursday, March 20, 1872 and Preached on the Lord's Day Following'.

Give thanks that your life is in the hands of a good God who oversees his world. In times of suffering, this can be especially mind-boggling and heart-wrenching to comprehend. But it means God is using even these seasons to grow us in Christlikeness, and to display his sovereign kindness to us, in us and through us – for all eternity. How does this change how you face the coming day?

Listen to *'Epiphany: Rejoice, All You!'* by Liturgical Folk, featuring Sandra McCracken.

It Doesn't Get Better than Boaz

Read Ruth 2:4–9

EVERYBODY LOVES A BABY!

Sometimes Christians can struggle with worshipping a Saviour who arrives as a baby. After all, newborn babies aren't renowned for having much personality! Imagine an older child who, on seeing everyone fussing over their new sibling, says, 'But it's just a baby!'

Perhaps we wonder how we can really worship someone whose character we don't see at Christmas. If so, today's passage in Ruth might help us...

FIRST IMPRESSIONS

You only get one chance to make a first impression. Boaz, Naomi's distant relative, does not disappoint: 'Just then Boaz arrived from Bethlehem and greeted the harvesters, "The LORD be with you!" "The LORD bless you!" they answered' (v. 4). What an entrance!

We've been told Boaz is a 'man of standing' (v. 1), but this is evidently more than power and wealth. How many employers greet their workforce like Boaz does? And how many get such a hearty response in return?

See too how Boaz's first words aren't drawing attention to himself or ushering commands to his workforce. He speaks first and foremost of the Lord, hardly a common trait at this point in Israel's history.

HE'S THE MAN!

Boaz then spots a new face in his field and asks who does this girl 'belong to' (v. 5). This may seem an odd phrase to us, but Boaz is essentially checking that Ruth has someone taking care of her.

And compare how Boaz speaks of Ruth to how his workers describe her. Boaz's manager speaks about Ruth as if she is 'one of them', highlighting her Moabite heritage (v. 6). But Boaz speaks *directly* to Ruth, with words full of dignity, care and gentleness: 'My daughter, listen to me...' (v. 8). (This probably also suggests Boaz was older than Ruth.)

Consequently, Boaz urges Ruth to stay, and he promises she'll be safe and looked after (v. 9). As we might say, this is the kind of man you'd take home to your mother – and I'm sure Naomi would agree!

JOY OF EVERY LONGING HEART

We know this was a time when God's people really needed a king (Judges 21:25; Ruth 1:1), but we know the *character* of this king mattered even more.

In Boaz, we're being given the profile of all that a leader could be. This is a man who takes God's word seriously (for example, about gleaning); treats individuals with dignity; speaks unashamedly of God; and offers provision and protection to others. Why would we look any further than Boaz?

And for us as Christians, this points us forward to King Jesus, who perfectly 'colours in' Boaz's outline. A dip into any of the gospels shows us Jesus' kind and gracious kingship. Yes, Boaz shows us Christlike character, but he also gives us a glimpse of Christ himself.

Spend some time marvelling at Boaz's character, then 'look through Boaz' to his great-great-great-(and so on)-grandson, Jesus, and compare him with some of the leadership we see in the world around us. How much do you consider the character of Jesus at Christmas? Whilst worshipping a baby may seem strange, knowing his character shows us why he's worth making a fuss over!

 Listen to *'Come Thou Long Expected Jesus'* by Shane and Shane.

Why Jesus Is
Better than Santa

Read Ruth 2:10–13

HE'S MAKING A LIST...

A couple of years ago, a video did the rounds on social media of a young boy getting warned by his dad that his bad behaviour would put him on Santa's naughty list. The kid gets visibly affronted by this and responds with comical indignation: 'Well, Father Christmas is not being very nice to me!'

Whether or not your household 'does Santa' (I'm not opening that can of worms!), many people imagine God as a kind of cosmic Father Christmas. Perhaps we feel we need to be on our best behaviour because otherwise God will 'find out who's naughty or nice'.

But thankfully, the gospel is much better than Santa – and Ruth chapter 2 is going to help us see why!

WHY WOULD YOU NOTICE ME?

God has led Ruth to Boaz's field, where she has encountered his stunning generosity. In response, Ruth asks Boaz a question, which takes us to the heart of the gospel. Bowing her face in humble disbelief, Ruth asks, 'Why have I found such favour in your eyes that you notice me – a foreigner?' (v. 10).

It's sometimes said that we live in an 'entitlement generation'. Look at the way that Christmas lists turn into Christmas *demands*, or how festive gatherings can quickly boil over as someone takes offence at the slightest remark.

And maybe this entitlement can spill over into how we approach *God*.

But not so with Ruth. For a start, she knew she was at the bottom rung of the ladder in terms of her cultural social standing: a widow, a foreigner and, worst of all, a Moabite. She was an outsider to God's covenant promises and so she bows her face (v. 10).

So why *had* Boaz noticed her? Boaz's answer seems intriguing. He acknowledges how Ruth has treated Naomi (v. 11) and then he blesses her, 'May the LORD repay you for what you have done' (v. 12).

Is Boaz suggesting Ruth has *earned* his kindness, a bit like how we think about Santa? Is Boaz just rewarding Ruth's actions with bundles of grain, rather than sacks of coal?

MEEK SOULS WILL RECEIVE HIM STILL

Boaz is pointing out that ultimately Ruth has received blessing because she's turned and trusted in the Lord. His description of Ruth's actions even evokes memories of Abraham's faith (v. 11).

And don't miss the wonder of Boaz's final remark: 'May you be richly rewarded by the LORD, the God of Israel, under whose wings you have come to take refuge' (v. 12). It's the imagery of a baby bird seeking protection under the wings of their parent. But, of course, in such a scenario we praise the provision and security of the parent rather than the efforts of the juvenile!

Likewise, Ruth has humbly come in repentance and faith to the Lord. Consequently, she is now enjoying a taste of the gracious blessing found under his wings. As such, we praise God for *his* kindness, rather than pat ourselves on the back.

These wings of refuge find their ultimate fulfilment in Jesus Christ. As we humbly come to him, turning and trusting in his mercy alone, we find a safe and secure place – even amidst the craziness of Christmas. Spend some time reflecting on how the gospel is much better than Santa! Are you ever tempted to try and prove your own worthiness instead?

Listen to *'The Unbelievable'* by Sovereign Grace Music.

11 DECEMBER

Contagious Kindness

Read Ruth 2:14–16

KINDNESS AROUND THE TABLE

The Christmas meal table has always been a powerful symbol of love and kindness. Think of that famous scene in Dickens's *Christmas Carol*, where Bob Cratchit invites Scrooge into his family home. Think of the scramble to fit extra chairs around a jam-packed table as family and friends gather together. Think of church members and charities opening their doors on Christmas Day to cook for strangers, such as the homeless, lonely neighbours, or international students away from home. Maybe you have lasting memories of being warmly welcomed into someone's home at Christmas?

In today's passage, a few hours have passed since Boaz was first introduced to Ruth. Presumably, since then Ruth has continued to work hard, gleaning in Boaz's field alongside his workers (v. 7), all the while safe in the knowledge that he has promised her protection.

But now, it is time for all the workers to pause and have refreshment. And whilst the work has halted, we're about to see that the kindness of God certainly hasn't.

KINDNESS WITH LEFTOVERS

Ruth has no expectation of eating with the others at this point. After all, she isn't an employee.

And yet Boaz welcomes Ruth: 'Come over here...' (v. 14). Rather than being left on the outside, she has been welcomed to the table.

There is bread and wine vinegar available, and then she is offered roasted grain too. Who knows when Ruth last had a meal of this quality or quantity!

The narrator tells us that Ruth 'ate all she wanted and had some left over' (v. 14). It's a spectacular display of abundance: far more than Ruth needed and could have imagined.

We've already seen how Boaz's provision and protection gives us a glimpse of Jesus Christ. As we read of the ample leftovers here, though, our minds might recall the abundant surplus when Jesus miraculously fed thousands (see, for example, Matthew 14:20; 15:37).

KINDNESS OVERFLOWS

Then, just as Ruth prepares to get back to work, Boaz says three things that should bowl us over in amazement. Firstly, he orders his men to allow Ruth to gather from the prime spot in his field ('among the sheaves'); secondly, he warns anyone against mistreating her; and thirdly, he even tells his men to 'pull out some stalks for her from the bundles and leave them for her to pick up' (v. 16).

It's an almost comical scene! Boaz's men would have been literally dropping their harvest on to the ground, with Ruth following behind picking it up!

Kindness is a recurring theme in this little book – demonstrated especially through Boaz and Ruth. And as we see such kindness in action, it's meant to wake up our hearts to the kindness of the Lord.

As we appreciate someone's kindness, it begins to soften and captivate us. In future reflections, we'll consider how we can be intentional with kindness. But first we need to warm our own hearts at the fire of Jesus' kindness to us. Imagine yourself in today's scene, welcomed to the table to eat and drink until your heart is full. Jesus welcomes us to himself, giving us his own body and blood to feed our hearts. This is lavish kindness.

Listen to *'Gift of Love'* by Melanie Penn.

12 DECEMBER

Grace upon Grace

Read Ruth 2:17–19a

WOULD YOU BELIEVE IT?

Ruth has found favour in the eyes of Boaz and now she returns to Naomi after probably the strangest day of her life. But as she's reunited with her mother-in-law, the spotlight of the narrative is firmly not on *them*, but on everything that Ruth brings back with her.

The amount of barley that Ruth has gleaned is about an 'ephah' (v. 17). Some Bible footnotes suggest this is perhaps as much as 13 kilograms. Whilst we don't know precisely, the point is that clearly it was loads!

Notice the way the narrator keeps drawing our eyes to Ruth's harvest: she carries 'it' home; Naomi sees 'how much she had gathered'; then Ruth also pulls out 'what she had left over' from her lunch with Boaz (v. 18). In other words, there's a growing mountain of food that Ruth has placed before Naomi!

ABOVE AND BEYOND

As we saw previously, the Old Testament law commanded landowners to allow widows, orphans and foreigners to glean at the edges of their fields for leftover scraps. In a sense, that was a display of grace. But what we see here is so far beyond what was expected or commanded. *This* is grace upon grace upon grace.

In this book, Boaz and Ruth are both living embodiments of the Lord's graciousness to Naomi. Here, the focus is on the abundant generosity of Boaz, but we've already seen the way *Ruth* promises to be committed to Naomi – even until her own body lies in the ground (1:16–17).

The clear implication throughout these chapters is that *both* Boaz and Ruth know the character of the Lord. He is a God who is defined by loving kindness (Exodus 34:6–7). Just as Naomi learns to trust in that gracious character, we're invited to trust in God's graciousness too.

GRACIOUSNESS RECONSIDERED

As we experience God's love, it begins to transform us. That's what has already happened to Ruth and Boaz. Likewise, we too are challenged as to whether we're displaying the character of the God we know and love.

Of course, being spiritually transformed doesn't work like a vending machine. We don't programme in God's graciousness and then out comes the character of graciousness in return. As we saw yesterday, it's only as our hearts are warmed by God's graciousness to us, that greed, pride and self-obsession will slowly be melted away.

The seventeenth-century pastor Richard Sibbes advised Christians that if we want to keep our hearts tender towards God and others, we should 'be always under the sunshine of the gospel'.[4] We're to meditate upon and marinate in the graciousness of God shown to us in Christ.

How much do you value graciousness in your life? What would today look like if you did value it? Perhaps you would be more gracious with the kids when they're grouchy, or with a seemingly inconsiderate work

---

[4] Richard Sibbes, sermon on 2 Chronicles 34:26, 'The Tender Heart', in *The Works of Richard Sibbes*, Volume 6, p. 41.

colleague or friend or spouse? And what about being gracious with those who are 'the least and the lost' in your community and across the world?

Listen to *'O Come, O Come, Emmanuel'* by Rain for Roots, featuring Sandra McCracken and Skye Peterson.

Hope Bursting Through

Read Ruth 2:19b–20

WHODUNNIT?

Throughout this chapter, Ruth has been on the receiving end of Boaz's spectacular kindness. But at *this* point in the story, Ruth doesn't yet know what we know: that this Boaz is actually a relative of her dead father-in-law (2:1)!

Similarly, whilst Naomi can see that Ruth has hit the jackpot gleaning in the fields of Bethlehem, she doesn't yet know who is the source of this rich blessing. Consequently, she eagerly asks Ruth, 'Where did you glean today? Where did you work? Blessed be the man who took notice of you!' (v. 19).

Delightfully for us as readers, it's only in today's passage that they both 'join the dots' – and so the extent of the Lord's loving providence dawns upon them both.

JOINING THE DOTS

Even as Ruth reveals the name of the man who has looked after her, she's herself none the wiser to its significance (v. 19). Maybe Ruth would be wondering if Naomi has even heard of this guy.

But obviously Naomi has! As she hears Ruth utter his name, Naomi is awestruck, exclaiming, 'The Lord bless him!' (v. 20).

Unsurprisingly, this reaction requires an explanation for Ruth. And so Naomi spells it out for her: 'That man is our close relative; he is one of our guardian-redeemers' (v. 20).

COULD THIS BE OUR REDEEMER?

This phrase 'guardian-redeemer' was a technical term. It described a male member of the wider family who was obliged to 'rescue' a relative if they got into a predicament.

As we've seen previously, this act of 'redeeming' was built into Old Testament law. For example, a dead man's brother would act as a 'redeemer' by marrying his brother's widow. This would be a commitment to provide for her and, if necessary, to seek to produce an heir to continue the dead man's family line.

Every male family member was therefore a potential redeemer. As Paul Miller puts it, redeeming was more than providing advice or finances. A redeemer was to actually 'own the problem'.[5] Redeeming love was a sacrificial decision to take the other person's helplessness upon yourself.

GRACE THAT DARES US TO HOPE

For Naomi, a glimmer of hope has now burst through into her helplessness. Although she probably knew of Boaz's existence, perhaps she assumed her own wandering past, not to mention Ruth's 'foreigner' status, would put Boaz off from getting involved. Now, as she hears of Boaz's lavish kindness, she dares to hope again.

For what if Boaz's actions were motivated by more than him just taking a fancy to Ruth? What if they're an initial indication that he might be willing to redeem his dead relative's family? Judging by Naomi's comment, she seems to think so. She concludes, 'He has not stopped showing his kindness to the living *and the dead*' (v. 20, my italics; the literal meaning here is: 'he does not *abandon…*').

But there is a delightful ambiguity to Naomi's comment too. Who is the 'he' that she is talking about? Instinctively, we think of Boaz,

---

5. Paul Miller, *A Loving Life*, p. 111.

and yet we can't help but also see that it is the Lord who is at work through these events. He does not abandon his people, whether in life or in death.

> Do you remember when you first glimpsed the gracious character of God? He has not stopped showing kindness to his people – and we'll still be enjoying his lavish grace into eternity. Even the grave does not stop his kindness. He takes our helplessness upon himself. Take a moment to reflect on his character and 'dare to hope' again.
>
> 🎵 Listen to *'Come Light Our Hearts'* by Sandra McCracken.

Actively Going Nowhere

Read Ruth 2:21–23

WHERE DOES YOUR HEART GO?

One of the phrases Christians often use at this time of year is 'Jesus is the reason for the season'. It can be a helpful reminder that in the midst of everything else, our hearts are meant to be captivated by the wonder of our newborn king!

And yet it's amazing how easily our hearts are drawn elsewhere in the Christmas season. We are drawn to the shiny shopping displays and bright websites that seek to persuade us their products will complete our lives. We are drawn to the idea of putting on a 'perfect Christmas' and so receiving the admiration of those we care about. We are drawn to the illusion of 'Christmas control', believing if we can just write enough lists and sort out enough jobs, then this year's celebrations will finally be everything we'd hoped.

As chapter 2 draws to a close, today's passage will invite us to consider what is captivating our hearts in this season.

WHY GO ANYWHERE ELSE?

Naomi has just been explaining to Ruth that Boaz is one of their family's 'guardian-redeemers'. Now, as Ruth and Naomi reflect on Ruth's encounter with this intriguing man, our narrator gives us three reminders as to where hope is to be found.

Firstly, Ruth explains that Boaz has encouraged her to stay with his workers until the harvest is over (v. 21). Secondly, Naomi responds to Ruth by stating her own recommendation that staying with Boaz will be 'good for you' (v. 22). Thirdly, we're told that Ruth does indeed follow this advice: she 'stayed close' to Boaz's party until the harvest was over (v. 23).

STATING THE OBVIOUS

Reading everything that's happened so far, the decision to stay in Boaz's field might seem a fairly obvious decision! After all, why would Ruth go anywhere else? As Naomi has said, the prospects from gleaning elsewhere were at best uncertain and at worst dangerous (v. 22).

And yet how often our hearts wander from treasuring Christ. Making 'obvious' decisions isn't quite so simple when our hearts are involved. As the hymnwriter Robert Robinson puts it, 'Prone to wander, Lord I feel it; prone to leave the God I love'.[6]

One of the reasons why we have a Christian calendar – and why we mark Advent and Christmas each year – is because a rhythm of following the gospel story helps us to keep reorientating our hearts on Christ. He is the place where true and lasting hope is to be found.

Where is your heart tempted to wander at this time of year? Where do you seek after satisfaction or hope? What has been captivating your daydreams or dominating your to-do lists? Remind your own heart about how good it is to remain with your Redeemer, and turn back to him in prayer now.

Listen to *'Gather Round, Ye Children, Come'* by Andrew Peterson.

---

6. Taken from Robert Robinson's hymn, 'Come, Thou Fount of Every Blessing' (1758).

Audacious Faith Flows from Certain Kindness

Read Ruth 3:1–5

YOU WANT ME TO DO WHAT?

Time has passed since Ruth's remarkable encounter in Boaz's field ('One day', v. 1). The fields are now empty and the harvest is over. Naomi knows she must find a *lasting* solution to their predicament. So having seen Boaz's kindness and knowing he is a relative, Naomi boldly hatches a plan to bring Ruth and Boaz together – and it's one that raises the eyebrows!

Naomi instructs Ruth, 'Wash, put on perfume, and get dressed in your best clothes' (v. 3). Next, Naomi tells Ruth to approach Boaz whilst he is sleeping, uncover his legs, lie down beside him – and then wait for Boaz's instructions (v. 4)!

This proposal seems more in keeping with a seductress in some steamy Hollywood blockbuster than the actions of a woman of God! What exactly does Naomi *expect* to happen when Boaz wakes up?

TONIGHT IS THE NIGHT?

But if we're surprised by Naomi's scheming, then Ruth's response is also astonishing. Willingly and emphatically, she commits to the plan: 'I will do whatever you say' (v. 5)! What on earth are we to make of this?

We're certainly meant to feel the sexual tension in the air. The verb 'to lie down' was associated with sexual activity and is used three times in quick succession (v. 4). Because of this, some writers suggest that Boaz and Ruth do 'get it on', a theory that casts a shadow on Naomi's wisdom and integrity.

Certainly, such a reading wouldn't seem out of place in both character's family trees. Boaz was a descendent of an unsavoury hook-up between an unsuspecting Judah and his disguised daughter-in-law Tamar (Genesis 38). As a Moabite, Ruth's origins came from an unaware and drunken Lot getting his own daughters pregnant (Genesis 19).

Yet what if that's to miss the whole point? Their background is what makes this chapter so stunning. Despite suggesting a charged atmosphere, our narrator is actually very careful *not* to indicate any impropriety. Our narrator can be crystal clear when we need to know sexual activity *has* occurred (4:13). As Ruth's actions tomorrow show, the power of this scene is actually that Ruth and Boaz break with their past and nothing untoward occurs. So if Naomi isn't encouraging a sexual encounter, what *is* she doing?

TAKING RISKS?

Let's remember Naomi's story. Experiences had left her sceptical about God's goodness. Returning to Bethlehem, she felt 'empty' (1:13, 21). But through Boaz's actions, it's as if she has begun to 'warm up' to the reality of God's love. Whereas previously she'd assumed 'rest' for Ruth would be found in Moab (1:9), now Naomi is looking to God to provide a lasting 'home' (3:1; literally, 'rest').

Here lies the motivation behind Naomi's elaborate instructions to Ruth. This isn't a desperate attempt to seduce Boaz by getting Ruth 'glammed up'. Quite the opposite! Naomi is encouraging Ruth to dress up as a prospective *bride*. Because Naomi has become utterly confident that God will provide a redeemer, she is now eager to encourage Boaz to be that redeemer and take Ruth as his wife. What might seem like a 'risky' move is actually an act of faith flowing from a trust in God's character.

It's sometimes said that when we're convinced that God's love is for us, then it's like an acrobat's harness. We're liberated to take seemingly risky, costly decisions for the sake of the gospel, knowing that God's love is steadfast. This was Naomi's experience and it's the same for us.

Audacious and expectant Christian faith grows when we bask in the steadfast kindness of God. Such faith is demonstrated the day we first 'count the cost' and turn to Christ, but it continues day-by-day, year-by-year. And it's a growing confidence in God's love that makes such lifelong trust in Christ a reality.

But will Ruth stick to the plan? And how will Boaz respond?

What were the seeming 'risks' when you first become a Christian? As you face up to the next few weeks – and even the year beyond – what 'risks' can you take for the sake of the gospel? As you learn from Naomi to put on the sure harness of God's love, what would audacious faith in God's gospel promises look like in your decision-making and prioritising?

Listen to *'O Come All Ye Faithful'* by Johnnyswim.

Bold I Approach

Read Ruth 3:6–9

CHRISTMAS COVER-UPS

One of the temptations that Christians can face at Christmas is to let the busyness of the season become an avoidance strategy for facing up to God ourselves. Even *Christian* busyness can become a way to 'cover ourselves', perhaps because deep down we're not really sure what God will make of us.

THE PLAN IN ACTION

Ruth keeps her promise to put Naomi's plan (3:3–5) into action. She follows Naomi's directions to the letter and approaches the threshing floor where Boaz lay.

As Christopher Ash points out, there's a beautiful symbolism here:

A threshing floor is the place where the wonderful potential of harvest begins to be realised, as the grain is threshed out, turning piles of cut stalks into mounds of life-giving grain.[7]

It's a scene brimming with hope and anticipation!

MANOEUVRES IN THE DARK

This is clearly a highly intimate moment. Exactly like we saw yesterday, the provocative verb 'to lie down' is used three times (vv. 7–8).

---

[7] Christopher Ash, *Teaching Ruth and Esther* (Christian Focus Publications, 2018), p. 93.

We can imagine Ruth tiptoeing over in the darkness as Boaz sleeps alone. In fact, it's so dark that Ruth and Boaz are simply described as 'the man' and 'a woman' (v. 8).

Quietly, Ruth uncovers Boaz's feet – presumably suggested by Naomi to gently wake him, just like when someone removes your duvet! What will Boaz make of this woman at his side? Is she a threat? A set-up? A prostitute? And so Boaz cries out, 'Who are you?' (v. 9).

But whilst Naomi had given Ruth fairly detailed instructions, she *hadn't* told Ruth how to identify herself! So what will Ruth say?

COVER ME

Reread Ruth's words again: 'I am your servant Ruth ... Spread the corner of your garment over me, since you are a guardian-redeemer of our family' (v. 9). This chapter began by showing us Naomi's faith, but now we see Ruth's too.

Earlier in the book, Ruth had identified herself to Boaz as an unworthy 'foreigner' (2:10), without 'the standing of one of your servants' (2:13). But Boaz has helped her to understand that having turned and trusted in God's mercy (1:16; 2:12), she is *now* under God's wings of refuge (2:12).

As such, Ruth makes a remarkable request. Even to reveal her identity is an act of boldness that breaks with the shadowy incognito encounters of Boaz and Ruth's ancestors in Genesis 19 and 38. But to boldly identify herself as *Boaz's* and to ask him to cover her (v. 9) is something else!

GRACE-FILLED WINGS OF REFUGE

Ruth's request is more than her simply asking Boaz to keep her warm! 'Corner' is the same Hebrew word as 'wings' and was often associated with marriage (see Ezekiel 16:6–14, especially v. 8). Just as Boaz had affirmed Ruth for coming under God's grace-filled wings (2:12), Ruth is now urging Boaz to likewise cover her with *his* wings (v. 9). In other words, dressed as a bride, Ruth has effectively proposed to Boaz!

But it is crucial for us to see that Ruth's striking boldness doesn't lie in *self*-confidence. Instead, it comes from a confidence in God's character, embodied in the kindness of Boaz himself.

And so Ruth's approach to Boaz gives us a glimpse of how we can relate to his greater descendant, Jesus. We can approach Christ with a humble boldness, knowing he is entirely willing to cover us. To put it another way, healthy spiritual confidence lies not in ourselves, but in the character of God, who graciously invites us under his 'wings of refuge'.

Do you ever turn to busyness and activity as a way of 'covering yourself' – perhaps to avoid facing up to God or even to yourself? What difference does it make to know that today we can 'approach God's throne of grace with confidence … and find grace to help us in our time of need' (Hebrews 4:16)?

Listen to *'The Perfect Gift'* by J.J. Heller.

She's the One!

Read Ruth 3:10–11

A GREATER KINDNESS?

We left yesterday on a cliffhanger. How will Boaz respond to Ruth's bold wedding proposal (v. 9)?

At first glance, Boaz's reply seems strange. Rather than commenting on Ruth's boldness, he focuses on her *kindness* (v. 10). Why? After all, surely *he* is the one we hope will show kindness – by marrying Ruth?

And yet Boaz sees astounding kindness in Ruth's actions: 'This kindness is greater than that which you showed earlier: you have not run after the younger men, whether rich or poor' (v. 10). So what exactly is this 'greater' kindness that Ruth has shown?

KIND TO WHOM?

We might assume Boaz means Ruth's kindness to *him*. After all, she's indicated a willingness to marry him – rather than any younger potential suitors.

But is that what Boaz means? Does that count as even 'greater' than the covenant love Ruth had previously shown to Naomi (1:16–17)?

Consider again Ruth's actions. She has followed Naomi's audacious plan to approach Boaz in the middle of the night (3:5). She has been willing to offer herself to Boaz in marriage, in order that Naomi's family is redeemed (3:9).

To whom has Ruth now shown a 'greater' kindness? To *Naomi*. This incident has powerfully demonstrated that Ruth is willing to use her life to provide an heir to Naomi and Elimelek, Naomi's dead husband.

Therefore, Boaz's comment about Ruth not running after 'younger men' (v. 10) is not so much about Ruth choosing Boaz over a 'younger model', but about Ruth choosing Naomi's future over her own preferences.

THE REAL LOVE STORY

We often think of this book as a love story between Boaz and Ruth. Actually, the book's real focus is on the deep covenant love Ruth shows to Naomi.

Wonderfully, Boaz then confirms he *is* willing to redeem them: 'I will do for you all you ask' (v. 11). But the clear emphasis here is on *Ruth's* actions moving Boaz's heart. He even says that the whole of Bethlehem has recognised her as 'a woman of noble character' (v. 11).

This is a very particular phrase. Firstly, it matches the earlier description of Boaz as 'a man of standing' (2:1), showing they're a perfect fit! But secondly, it's the same phrase famously used in Proverbs 31:10. And staggeringly, Ruth is the only woman in the whole Bible described as fitting the bill!

IF THE CAP FITS

Fascinatingly, the book of Proverbs (rather than the book of Judges) originally came immediately before Ruth. So Israelite readers would have read Proverbs' incredible description of the woman of 'noble character' and then seen her fleshed out in Ruth chapter 3. Yet *this* woman is a foreign, childless widow scavenging for scraps. That's hardly what we might imagine when reading Proverbs 31!

In fact, Proverbs 31 resonates with what we've seen of Ruth. She was a woman who 'laughs at the time to come' and who has 'kindness … on her tongue' (Proverbs 31:25–26, ESV). Against all preconceptions, it is this Moabite who embodies the dazzling beauty of kindness and a steady trust in God's providence.

As we journey through Ruth, we become captivated by the kindness of the characters in the story. And perhaps our thoughts go to another young woman who was willing to submit her life to God: Mary, the mother of Jesus. These women 'enflesh' the steadfast kindness of God for us, and in doing so, they give us a glimpse of Christ. Pray we'd do likewise!

Listen to *'Mary's Song'* by Robbie Seay Band.

18 DECEMBER

I Will Do It

Read Ruth 3:12–18

DON'T BE AFRAID

Yesterday, the spotlight of our passage fell on Ruth's stunning kindness to her mother-in-law, Naomi. Today, our narrator now highlights the wonder of Boaz's response to Ruth's request.

Imagine Ruth's heart beating rapidly in the darkness, waiting for Boaz's response. She had crept to this man's side in the middle of the night. There were no witnesses. No one would know what happened. Boaz could have done anything. People would say Ruth just had herself to blame.

But what does Boaz say? 'And now, my daughter, don't be afraid. I will do for you all you ask' (2:11). Boaz is willing to do the one thing Ruth hoped, dreamed, longed for him to do. And we see his tenderness of heart exemplified in the way he addresses her as 'daughter'.

We breathe a sigh of relief. Boaz is ready to be the redeemer of this troubled family.

THE TWIST

But there's a 'but'! Suddenly, we're given exasperating new information. Boaz explains that Naomi already has a closer male relative than himself (v. 12). As such, they must wait to see if this other man will 'do his duty' (v. 13) and choose to redeem Naomi.

We draw a deep breath. It was all going so well!

Yet even this moment showcases Boaz's integrity. Rather than abuse or shame Ruth, he honours her (helping her go home without being seen, v. 14), as well as honouring his own unnamed relative. Of course, in doing both of these, Boaz also honours God.

And all the while, Boaz again provides for Ruth and Naomi, filling Ruth's shawl with barley. Naomi, who once felt 'empty' (1:21), now ends another chapter without being 'empty-handed' (v. 17; see also 2:18). Boaz truly is a 'man of standing' (2:1).

LET ME GO THERE

In R.S. Thomas's short Advent poem *The Coming*, the Welsh writer imagines the Father holding our world in his hands and inviting the Son to look at humanity in all our mess and brokenness. The poem closes with these precious words: 'The Son watched them. Let me go there, he said.' It's a moving depiction of all that we celebrate at Christmas: the eternal Son of God willingly stepping into our world in order to save us.

But Thomas could have written a very similar poem about Boaz as he looks upon Ruth and Naomi. *Let me go there* '... I will do it' (v. 13). Again, we find ourselves looking through Boaz and seeing *Jesus*. We have a gentle, tender Redeemer who again and again in the gospels says, to the least and the lowly, 'Don't be afraid' (see, for example, Matthew 10:31; 14:27; 17:7; Mark 5:36; 6:50; Luke 5:10; 8:50; 12:7; John 6:20).

Jesus will do it. He *has* done it.

As you face the broken realities of our world and your own life, how does it feel to know that Jesus looked at them and said, 'I will do it'? How does that help you not to be 'afraid' at the darkness and hopelessness of our lives? Give thanks, rejoicing in this willing Redeemer.

 Listen to '*Maker, Made a Child*' by Emu Music.

Signed, Sealed, Delivered

Read Ruth 4:1–4

LOVE RECONSIDERED

How do you *know* that God loves you? Right now, in the middle of the craziness of Christmas preparations, how do you *really* know that God loves you?

How we answer that question will depend on how we understand love. Whilst there are glorious exceptions, *generally* our culture defines love as feeling and emotion. We feel it in our fingers, feel it in our toes, as Billy Mack's spoof song 'Christmas Is All Around' put it. We 'fall in love' and 'fall out of love'.

But today, we're going to see that God's love is a very different kind of love...

BOAZ MEANS BUSINESS

As the day-after-the-night-before dawns, we now find ourselves at Bethlehem's 'town gate' (v. 1), where legal decisions were made. This is a very different scene from yesterday! The intimate language of 'lying down' (3:4, 7–8) has been replaced with the formal language of 'sitting down' (vv. 1–2). But we're here *because* of love. Boaz won't rest until Naomi and Ruth's predicament is resolved (3:18).

And, would you believe it, who should Boaz spot but Naomi's closer relative, the potential 'guardian-redeemer'. The 'just as' phrasing here (v. 1) is the same as when Ruth found herself in Boaz's field ('as it turned out', 2:3). The same sovereign God is working behind the scenes.

Boaz means business, so he directs the relative to sit down (v. 1) and quickly gathers ten elders to act as necessary witnesses (v. 2).

A LEGAL REDEMPTION

What's this scene all about? Every Israelite family had a plot of land that would be passed down the generations as a marker of their share in God's promises. But when Naomi and her husband left Bethlehem, probably either they sold their family land or someone else took it over.

Now that Naomi is back in the promised land, it seems she can only get the family land back if someone redeems it on her behalf, in turn providing for her as well. As we've seen, the responsibility to do this lay upon the closest relative, and so Boaz addresses this unnamed man: 'If you will redeem it, do so' (v. 4).

MR RIGHT?

Not for the first time in Ruth, we hold our breath! But then the man speaks: 'I will redeem it' (v. 4).

On paper, it probably seemed a good deal. Naomi's land would generate extra income, most likely more than covering the cost of looking after an ageing woman. Yet it's a heart-in-the-mouth moment for us. Of course, we wanted Boaz to be the guardian-redeemer!

LEGAL LOVE?

We'll have to wait to see what happens next, but take a moment to reflect on this 'business scene'. Maybe this 'legal stuff' seems a bit technical? But in the Bible, God's covenant love is bound up with a legal commitment. It's not just an emotion or a momentary feeling. It's the difference between 'I'll do it right now, whilst I feel like it' and

'I will do it, because I've promised'. To be sure of God's love when circumstances are hard, we need a Redeemer who has signed on the dotted line.

> *The apostle Paul says this: 'God sent his Son, born of a woman, born under the law, to redeem those under the law, that we might receive adoption to sonship' (Galatians 4:5). Jesus' love doesn't depend on our feelings. He gives his life to ensure an unchangeable legal commitment. Give thanks for a Redeemer who did everything necessary to redeem us.*
>
> Listen to *'Lift Your Eyes (Come Adore)'* by Sheffield Collective.

The Cost of Christmas

Read Ruth 4:5–6

PAYING THE PRICE

With newsfeeds, TV screens and magazines all seeking to persuade us to spend our cash on advertisers' festive products, it's no wonder that we often lament the 'cost of Christmas'. But most people don't ever give much thought to what the first Christmas cost the one person it's all about...

WHO WILL REDEEM?

We've been left on tenterhooks after Naomi's unnamed relative said he would do his duty and redeem Naomi. But wait...

Boaz is not done. Perhaps shrewdly, he points out what Naomi's relative might have missed:

> On the day you buy the land from Naomi, you also acquire Ruth the Moabite, the dead man's widow, in order to maintain the name of the dead with his property (v. 5).

Ah, hang on... It seems this man hasn't quite factored in everything. By the way, the language of 'acquiring' here isn't to demean Ruth, as if she were merely a possession. It actually highlights her dignity and right to receive care.

But the man will not only need to care for Ruth. Boaz makes clear the redeemer will also be expected to maintain the name and line of

Elimelek, Naomi's dead husband. The implication is that the man would need to marry Ruth and provide an heir for Elimelek.

DEAL-BREAKER!

We can imagine the man's eyebrows going up! Not only would there be extra mouths to feed (Ruth's plus those of any future children), but he would then have to pass on Naomi's land *to* those children. Then there's the fact his new wife would be a Moabite!

Suddenly, this doesn't seem a very lucrative deal. And so he says, 'Then I cannot redeem it because I might endanger my own estate. You redeem it yourself. I cannot do it' (v. 6).

At least there's no pretence here. The man is honest about this being too costly to his bank balance, his pride and his reputation. Ultimately that's not a price he's willing to pay.

And so we're back on with Boaz!

I'LL NEVER KNOW HOW MUCH IT COST

This twist doesn't just make for a more gripping story, but it also highlights how *costly* this redemption was. Boaz's *willingness* to redeem suddenly becomes all the more glorious in contrast to the other man's *unwillingness*. His sacrificial kindness shines all the brighter when set against a backdrop where the norm is self-preservation and 'looking after number one'.

We sometimes miss this cost of redemption in our culture. An individual can 'redeem themselves' after a fault or mistake. We might 'redeem' a voucher at the shops.

But in the Bible, redemption isn't something *we* can do. Humanity's enslavement to sin, death and the devil leaves us utterly unable to redeem ourselves – and desperately in need of a willing Redeemer.

In Zechariah's announcement of Jesus' birth, he says, 'Praise be to the Lord, the God of Israel, because he has come to his people and redeemed them' (Luke 1:68). The cost of this redemption was the Redeemer giving his own life. Whilst our redemption is free to us, it is only possible because Jesus Christ willingly paid the cost with his blood. What difference does it make to know that you have a Redeemer who paid the cost for our lives? Nothing or no one else has done that!

Listen to 'The Cradle and the Cross' by Austin Stone Worship.

Left without a Name

Read Ruth 4:7–10

STEP INTO MY SHOES

We're in for a dramatic end to this fascinating little book!

Naomi's closest relative has just turned down his right to buy her land (4:6), and so the opportunity has opened up to our hero Boaz (4:4). This means Ruth and Boaz might *finally* get together!

But in order to now 'seal the deal', a particular Israelite legal custom has to take place. The closest relative must remove their sandal and pass it to the new redeemer to wear (v. 7). As Christopher Ash explains, one person was forgoing their right to 'step' on the land, whilst the other was 'stepping into their shoes' and taking on the land.[8] Once he has done this, Boaz can say he's acquired 'all the property of Elimelek, Kilion and Mahlon' (v. 9), that is all that belonged to Naomi's dead husband and two sons (1:2).

Notice, though, what Boaz then emphasises:

I have also acquired Ruth the Moabite, Mahlon's widow, as my wife, in order to maintain the name of the dead with his property, so that his name will not disappear from among his family or from his home town (v. 10).

[8.] Christopher Ash, *Teaching Ruth and Esther*, p. 120.

THE LIVING AND THE DEAD

Why has Boaz willingly taken on the cost of caring for this family? Why has he shown such extraordinary kindness? He tells us that it's in order that Elimelek's name will not disappear but will continue to be associated with this land. In fact, some translations helpfully draw out the language of 'inheritance' here. For example, the NRSV reads: 'to maintain the dead man's name on his inheritance' (4:5, 10).

Staggeringly, Boaz's commitment stretches way back beyond Ruth to Naomi's dead husband, Elimelek.

LAND AHOY!

Why does it matter that Elimelek's land is passed on in his name?

Land is very significant in the book of Ruth, but we sometimes miss this as twenty-first-century Christians. Possessing land in Israel meant having a share in God's promises and blessing. After all, it was this land of blessing that had been first promised to Abraham (Genesis 12:7), before being divided between tribes and family clans (Joshua 13–21).

Everlasting life in God's kingdom also seems to be symbolically demonstrated in the Old Testament by a family line continuing to be associated with that land. Therefore, losing land, or having your name disassociated from the land, was a sign of being cut off from God's blessing. Yet, devastatingly, this is what had happened to Elimelek and his sons.

So it's a measure of Boaz's selfless kindness that he acts to reinclude Elimelek's name. Rather than doing as he 'saw fit', like many in Israel at the time (Judges 21:25; Ruth 1:1), Boaz instead honours God by serving his fellow Israelite.

THE ONE WHO GIVES US AN INHERITANCE

As the Bible unfolds, we see more clearly that God's inheritance is not simply land; it's God himself, come to 'dwell with them' (Revelation 21:3), our 'portion for ever' (Psalm 73:26).

But how do we receive this inheritance? At the cross, Jesus – our Boaz-like Redeemer – steps into our shoes, pays our debt and gives us all that he has. As we turn to and trust in him, we become bound up with him and his name.

As we marvel at Boaz's generosity, consider whose name you are seeking to maintain this Christmas. Are you moved by God's generosity to bless others? Rejoice in a Redeemer that includes us in his inheritance and pray that you might seek to make much of his name.

 Listen to *'Sing We the Song of Emmanuel'* by Matt Boswell and Matt Papa, featuring Keith and Kristyn Getty.

Ordinary Glory

Read Ruth 4:11–12

TINSEL MOMENTS

At Christmastime, it's easy for our attention to be grabbed by moments of Christmas 'glory': presents, parties, holidays. But as a result, we can sometimes rush past serving God in the mundane and everyday.

How might the book of Ruth speak into this? As the whole community gathers around Boaz, Ruth and Naomi, they respond with three extraordinary prayers to God (vv. 11–12)!

JOINING THE LEGENDS

Firstly, they pray for Ruth: 'May the LORD make the woman who is coming into your home like Rachel and Leah, who together built up the family of Israel' (v. 11).

Rachel and Leah together bore eight of the founding fathers of the tribes of Israel (Genesis 29–30). But to mention Ruth in the same breath seems remarkable. This is a *Moabite*, who had previously been married for ten years without conceiving (1:4–5)!

A MAN OF RENOWN

Next, they pray for Boaz: 'May you have standing in Ephrathah and be famous in Bethlehem' (4:11).

The elders had just witnessed a remarkable display of Boaz's character. Whilst Boaz was already a 'man of standing' (2:1), they pray

Boaz's 'standing' increases across his wider family clan, Ephrathah, based in Bethlehem.

As we'll see, Boaz's name would indeed never be forgotten under Bethlehem skies.

FROM AUDACIOUS ACORNS...

Lastly, they pray for the fruit of Boaz and Ruth's marriage: 'Through the offspring the LORD gives you by this young woman, may your family be like that of Perez, whom Tamar bore to Judah' (v. 12).

Perez was from the royal tribe of Judah, but his birth was surrounded in controversy. His mother, Tamar, had been abandoned by her dead husband's family. It was actually Tamar's father-in-law, Judah, who unknowingly fathered Perez, after Tamar boldly disguised herself as a prostitute and Judah slept with her (Genesis 38:8–30).

But as Paul Miller puts it, 'If God can use Tamar's feistiness to make her the mother of the tribe of Judah, what will God do with Ruth's *hesed*?'[9]

GLORY OF THE ORDINARY

Ruth is a much-loved book, but there's something very *ordinary* about it. Ruth was a nobody and her only Israelite relative, Naomi, was a bereft and broken widow.

But that 'ordinariness' is actually why this story is so precious. As our three characters get caught up in the Lord's covenant kindness, we find significance and glory in their 'ordinariness'. At the same time, today's three prayers highlight how their trust in God and their remarkable kindness make them worthy of comparison with the greats of Israel's history.

Fast-forward a thousand years and we find another very ordinary girl in Bethlehem: a pregnant teenager, engaged to a carpenter,

---

[9.] Paul Miller, *A Loving Life*, p. 148.

miles from home. Yet as she and her fiancé submit their lives to the Lord, they are also swept up in a glory far beyond anything they imagined.

Frederick Buechner writes,

> *If holiness and the awful power and majesty of God were present in this least auspicious of all events, this birth of a peasant's child, then there is no place or time so lowly and earthbound that holiness cannot be present there too.*[10]

Rejoice that our ordinary lives have been graciously caught up in the Lord's story of redemption. Pray that we'd delight to submit our 'ordinary' lives to God and display his kindness in the everyday.

 Listen to *'Under Bethlehem Skies'* by Paul Bell.

---

[10] Frederick Buechner, 'A Face in the Sky – Christmas Day' in *Secrets in the Dark: A Life in Sermons* (HarperCollins, 2006).

Who Would Have Dreamed?

Read Ruth 4:13–15

IT'S ALL ABOUT THE BABY

Birth announcements are big business these days: baby scan photos, gender reveal balloons, elaborate Facebook statuses. But today, in Ruth, we have an altogether different birth announcement.

The last half of the book has been an exciting 'will-they-won't-they' build-up to the coming together of Ruth and Boaz. Yet with seeming breakneck speed (spot the five verbs in quick succession in verse 13!), we rush past the wedding celebration, straight past the consummation and so quickly discover the narrator's real interest: 'the LORD enabled [Ruth] to conceive, and she gave birth to a son' (v. 13). It's all about the *baby*.

UNTO US A SON IS GIVEN

Only twice in Ruth does the narrator describe 'the LORD' (Exodus 34:6–7) doing something. Each one is significant and together they bookend the story. The first occurs when the Lord ends the famine and provides bread for his people (1:6). The second comes here, as the Lord enables Ruth to conceive (v. 13).

Boaz was probably at least a generation older than Ruth, and we know Ruth had no children from the ten years of her first marriage. *Yet* the Lord provides a child.

And so the women of Bethlehem burst forth in praise. They remember when 'empty' and unrecognisable Naomi returned heartbroken to Bethlehem (1:19). Now, they celebrate that the Lord hasn't left Naomi 'without a guardian-redeemer' (v. 14).

But hang on, why this focus on 'a guardian-redeemer'? Have they started talking about Boaz again? What about the baby?

THE REDEEMER IS HERE

As we ponder the women's words, though, we see it is very much the baby they have in mind: 'For your daughter-in-law, who loves you and who is better to you than seven sons, has given *him* birth' (v. 15, my italics).

Of course, what Boaz did was incredibly noble, but only an heir could secure Naomi and Elimelek's family line and inheritance. Now that this heir has been born, the party can really start!

Just look at this baby's job description: 'He will renew your life and sustain you in your old age' (v. 15). The word 'renew' here is the same as 'return', used repeatedly in chapter 1. Just as the Lord had 'returned' Naomi to the promised land, this child reconnects Naomi into an everlasting inheritance that 'returns' her life to her.

KINDNESS ENFLESHED IN KINDNESS

Read verse 15 again and note how the women, with a moving display of respect to this baby's mother, highlight Ruth's role in Naomi's life: 'For your daughter-in-law, who loves you and who is better to you than seven sons, has given him birth' (v. 15).

Nowhere else in this book is the verb 'to love' used. Without a doubt, Ruth's love for her mother-in-law is the real love story.

The fact that Ruth is worth more than 'seven sons' is quite something given we've just celebrated a son! But this has been Naomi's surprising journey of discovery: finding the Lord's extravagant loving kindness 'enfleshed' in the most unexpected of places, her Moabite daughter-in-law.

At Christmas, we see the supreme example of God's kindness 'enfleshed', as God the Son takes on human flesh, the true God of true God becoming fully human in order to love us beyond compare. Take some time to join your praises with those of the women in Bethlehem, for the Lord has not left us without a Redeemer. He will renew our life, even beyond the grave.

Listen to 'Who Would Have Dreamed?' by Sovereign Grace Music.

24 DECEMBER

Naomi's Noel

Read Ruth 4:16–22

BABE IN ARMS

We sometimes use the old word 'Noel' at Christmastime, meaning the good news of a joyful birth. It's a fitting word for the end of this book too.

Naomi, the woman who lost her husband and both her sons, is now holding a young boy in her arms. This indeed is a glorious Noel! Beautifully, the Hebrew word for 'child' (literally, 'young lad', v. 16) was last used when we were told, 'Naomi was left without her two young sons [that is, lads]' (1:5). Now, she has a young lad *again* – and what a journey it's been!

WHOSE SON?

In fact, as Naomi holds her grandson, we may find the onlookers' comment a little strange: 'Naomi has a son!' (v. 17). Isn't this *Ruth's* boy?

But this is the whole point. The spotlight falls on Naomi to show us how *her* situation has been completely reversed.

Once 'empty' (1:21), now her lap is filled with blessing. Twice she's found herself surrounded by piles of grain that Boaz has given to Ruth (2:18; 3:17). Now, God has provided not just fruit of the land, but fruit of the womb. Her heir is here and her emptiness has been turned to fullness. There is an everlasting light that shines, even in the darkest of nights.

GLORY TO THE NEWBORN KING

But even this is no ordinary child. Named Obed, we're told he becomes 'the father of Jesse, the father of David' (v. 17). This book began with a reminder that it was the time of judges (1:1), when 'Israel had no king; everyone did as they saw fit' (Judges 21:25). Now, we have a child born who will be the grandfather of Israel's great king, David!

And so God has been at work on a level far greater than simply one family. Just as the Lord provided bread to end Bethlehem's famine, just as he provided a redeemer to end Ruth and Naomi's emptiness, so the Lord has provided a child to end the desperate need of God's people for a king.

As John Piper puts it, 'This simple little story opens out like a stream into an ocean of hope.'[11] We step back and see the epic vistas of God's salvation plan – and it truly is glorious.

COME AND SEE WHAT GOD HAS DONE

Of course, as we'll hardly need reminding, King David was not the end of the story. David's line weaves down through history to Bethlehem's most famous son, Jesus of Nazareth – but more on that tomorrow. Every powerful lesson and glorious truth displayed in this precious book of Ruth ends up being magnified, for the 'fullness' of God's kind provision is even greater than Ruth, Boaz and Naomi could have ever imagined. As the hymn 'O Come, All Ye Faithful' proclaims, 'O come let us adore him, Christ the Lord.'[12]

I hope you'll agree that Ruth is a glorious book for Advent.

---

[11] John Piper, *A Sweet and Bitter Providence* (IVP, 2009), p. 108.

[12] Taken from John Wade's hymn, 'O Come, All Ye Faithful' (1743).

How have you felt as you've traced Naomi's journey through this book? How does she help you learn to trust in the Lord's good hand on your life? Step back from all the frantic activity of today and lift your eyes to the grand story of God's redemption plan for the world. Pray that today, tomorrow and always, your heart would be strengthened by knowing this King has come – for us.

Listen to *'Noel'* by Lauren Daigle and Chris Tomlin.

Merry Christmas!

Read Matthew 1:1–16

CATCHING YOUR BREATH

Christmas Day is an inevitably hectic day for many of us! And the story of Ruth has often gone at breakneck speed. So to wrap up *Finding Hope Under Bethlehem Skies*, we're going to celebrate Jesus' birth by briefly joining the dots from Ruth to Matthew's Gospel.

RUTH'S STORY, HIS STORY, OUR STORY

For the first readers of the book of Ruth, the family tree at the end of chapter 4 must have been fascinating. Having got to know Ruth, Naomi and Boaz, picture their reaction when discovering just where this family story ends up. The miraculous firstborn of this Moabite widow would become the grandfather of Israel's greatest king, David! Imagine if you'd tried telling that to Ruth and Naomi as they returned to Bethlehem back in chapter 1…

But as we read the opening to Matthew's Gospel, we see that King David isn't the end of the story either! David is just a hint of a much greater summit: 'Jesus who is called the Messiah' (Matthew 1:16).

As Matthew begins his account of Jesus' life, he traces Jesus' lineage all the way, through David, back to Abraham. God had promised Abraham that his offspring would be a blessing to the whole world, and now Matthew shows us how Jesus is the fulfilment of that promise.

QUITE THE FAMILY TREE

But as we make our journey from Abraham to Jesus, Matthew also makes a point of stopping off along the way in all kinds of intriguing places. And that's because he wants us to see the kinds of people Jesus' family history includes.

For starters, it was highly unusual to include any women – and yet Matthew goes out of his way to mention *five* (including Ruth, 1:5).

This certainly isn't a 'greatest hits' of Israel's history. As Ann Voskamp puts it, Jesus' arrival was 'through families of messed-up monarchs and battling brothers, through affairs and adultery and more than a feud or two, through skeletons in closets and cheaters at tables'.[13]

Neither are Jesus' ancestors restricted to being Israelites. In particular, Ruth was a Moabite. It's a clear indication that Jesus' heart would be for the *nations*. John Piper captures it like this: 'Just as his blood was shed for the nations, so the nations' blood ran in his veins.'[14]

FOR YOU AND ME

Perhaps our final encouragement, though, should be personal. The pastor Sam Allberry notes that this family tree highlights how the kind of people Jesus comes *from* anticipates the kind of people Jesus has come *for*.[15]

However our Christmas Day goes, whether it meets our expectations or whether the cracks appear far more quickly than we'd like, Jesus has come for *people like us*. Outsiders and oddballs. Sinners and sufferers and strangers. The wanderers and the weary. Heartbroken widows and hopeful daughters-in-law.

---

13. Ann Voskamp, https://religionnews.com/2013/12/10/nyt-bestseller-ann-voskamp-hung-christmas-tree-upside/

14. John Piper, *A Sweet and Bitter Providence*, p. 112.

15. Sam Allberry, http://twitter.com/samallberry/status/805079815342657536

He came down to earth from heaven,
Who is God and Lord of all,
And his shelter was a stable,
And his cradle was a stall;
With the poor and meek and lowly,
Lived on earth our Saviour holy.[16]

Give thanks to the Lord for the gift of Jesus, who rewrites our stories and writes us into his story. Pray that the wonder of this might dwell in your heart over this busy but special day.

 Listen to *'Matthew's Begats'* by Andrew Peterson.

---

[16] Taken from Cecil Alexander's hymn, 'Once in Royal David's City' (1848).